The Fun of Meeting Jesus

By the Author

Liberating Jesus

My Thomas

The Fun of Dying

The Fun of Staying in Touch

The Fun of Growing Forever

The Fun of Living Together

THE FUN OF MEETING JESUS

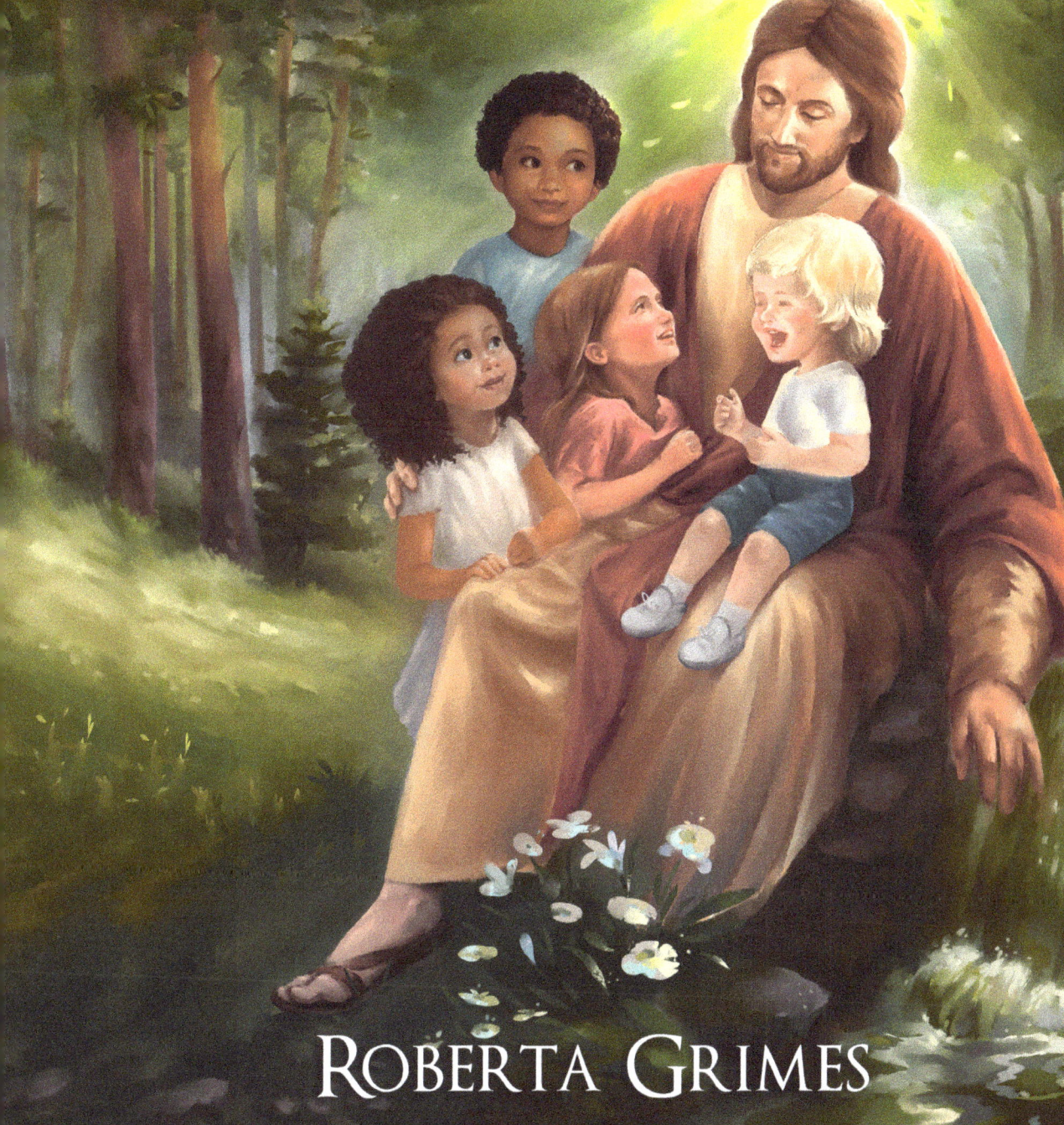

ROBERTA GRIMES

The Fun of Meeting Jesus by: Roberta Grimes

Copyright © 2021 by Roberta Grimes All rights reserved.

This book or part thereof may not be reproduced in any form, stored in a retrieval system, or transmitted in any form by any means—electronic, mechanical, photocopy, recording or otherwise— without prior written permission of the publisher, except as provided by United States of America copyright law.

The text of the *New American Standard Bible®* may be quoted and/or reprinted up to and inclusive of one thousand (1,000) verses *without express written permission of The Lockman Foundation,* providing the verses do not amount to a complete book of the Bible nor do the verses quoted account for more than 50% of the total work in which they are quoted.

"Scripture quotations taken from the New American Standard Bible®, Copyright © 1960, 1962, 1963, 1968, 1971, 1972, 1973, 1975, 1977, 1995 by The Lockman Foundation Used by permission." (www.Lockman.org)

Publisher's Cataloging-In-Publication Data
(Prepared by The Donohue Group, Inc.)
Names: Grimes, Roberta.
Title: The fun of meeting Jesus / by Roberta Grimes.
Description: Normal, IL, Greater Reality Publications | [1]] "Read-aloud picture book — ages 1–6 years." | Interest age level: 001–006. | Summary: Emme, Barry, Quentin, and Sarah venture into the Scary Woods and become lost. While trying to find their way, they are comforted when they meet Jesus Christ who teaches them about forgiveness, love, and God.
Identifiers: ISBN 978-1-7374107-6-8 (hardcover) | ISBN 978-1-7374107-7-5 (Kindle)
Subjects: LCSH: Jesus Christ—Juvenile fiction. | Missing children—Juvenile fiction. | God (Christianity)—Juvenile fiction. | Forgiveness—Juvenile fiction. | Love—Juvenile fiction. | CYAC: Jesus Christ—Fiction. | Lost children—Fiction. | God (Christianity)—Fiction. | Forgiveness—Fiction. | Love—Fiction. | LCGFT: Picture books.
Classification: LCC PZ7.1.G75 Fu 2021 (print) | LCC PZ7.1.G75 (ebook) | DDC [E]—dc23

GR

Greater Reality Publications, Normal, IL
www.greaterreality.com
800 690 4232

ISBN: 978-1-7374107-6-8

Printed in the United States of America

The Fun with Jesus Series

These books introduce young people to the Gospel teachings of Jesus on love, forgiveness, and spiritual growth. They are based only in the Gospel teachings and not in the dogmas of any religion, so even children with no faith tradition can enjoy and benefit from this series. The Gospel teachings are a system for achieving very rapid spiritual growth that is so simple that even children can follow it, and so effective that when we begin early in life to know and to live the Gospel teachings they can very much improve our whole lives.

"Permit the children to come to Me. Do not hinder them, for the kingdom of God belongs to such as these. Truly I say to you, whoever does not receive the kingdom of God like a child will not enter it at all."

—MK 10:14-15

Emme and Barry live by the Scary Woods.

Mommy and Daddy keep them safe with a big fence.

Quentin and Sarah live next door.

Quentin wants to play in the Scary Woods.

So one day Quentin opens the gate…

…and the others follow him out.

The Scary Woods are scary! Barry starts to cry.

They try to find a path, but there is no path.

They find a river in the Scary Woods.

They can't cross it. So they follow it.

Sarah and Barry are both crying now.

They want to stop. Emme takes their hands.

They come to a glen. A man is sitting there.

He says to them, "**Hello children! Come to me. Don't be afraid!**"

Quentin says, "We are lost. Can you help us?"

Emme says, "Who are you?"

The kind man says, "I am Jesus, the Son of Man. Come and sit with me, children. I love you as God loves you."

He smiles and comforts them with a hand on each head.

Sarah says, "We are lost! It is Quentin's fault!"

Jesus says to Sarah, "Quentin did not mean to make you lost. Forgive him. If you forgive others, then you will be forgiven when you make your own mistakes."

Emme says to Jesus, "Quentin is sorry! He wanted us to have fun. He did not mean to make us lost."

Jesus says, "Blessed are the peacemakers. They are doing God's work. Bless you, Emme, that you try to make peace!"

Jesus smiles at the children. He says, "Soon I will take you home. But first, let me help you grow in wisdom. All people should be as gentle as children, for the gentle will inherit the earth. The winner is not the one who fights! The winner is the one who lives in love and kindness."

"People are happiest when they make others happy. Happiest of all are the pure in heart! They live with God."

Quentin says to Jesus, "Who is God?"

Jesus says, "God is Love. God is Spirit. God is within you, Quentin. You will know God more as you grow."

Jesus says, "We must love God with all our hearts, just as God loves us. And God wants us to love all people! Love everyone as much as I love you."

Jesus is standing up now. He says to Quentin, "You are good to care for your sister and your friends. Be merciful to them. When you show others mercy, you bring mercy to yourself."

He adds, "Children, the words that I have spoken to you are from God! Remember them. They will help you to live your best life."

Jesus says, "Dear children, you are the light of the world! Be perfect, as your heavenly Father is perfect."

Emme says to Jesus, "Thank you for helping us! But will you go away? How can we ever see you again?"

Jesus says, "I am with you always. Seek me and you always will find me."

As the children wave goodbye to Jesus, He calls to them,

"Remember to forgive with your whole heart! Love everyone the way that I love you! Grow in wisdom, dear children. I am with you always!"

The children wave goodbye to Jesus, but only for a little while.

They never will be afraid of the woods again!

A Brief Message for Grownups

Helping Children Learn to be Good People

The Gospels are the books of the Christian Bible where the words of Jesus are reported. Matthew, Mark, Luke, and John contain spiritual teachings that turn out to be a powerful system for helping us become the very best people that we can be. Following the Gospel teachings makes us more loving and more forgiving. And it makes us happy! These teachings are attached to no religion, so they work no matter what religion we follow, and even if we have no religion at all.

The Gospel teachings work for us even if we are old when we begin them, but they are magical for children. They are simple and intuitive. They make sense, and they help children begin to feel wise and confident. ***The Fun of Meeting Jesus*** introduces the teachings of Jesus on forgiveness and love and helps young children begin to apply these teachings to their daily lives.

We parents differ in the ambitions and hopes that we have for our children, but all of us want to rear confident young people who treat others with kindness and respect. We want our children to care enough about our communities and about our planet to want to make a positive difference. And it turns out that the simplest and most effective way for us to rear such beautiful young people is to begin when they are small to help them apply to their lives the eternal teachings of Jesus.

Reading the Teachings as They Were First Spoken

Given that Jesus spoke Aramaic, and that his teachings were translated first into Greek and then into every other language, it would be a wonder if the words in a modern translation of the Gospels were even close to what Jesus actually said. It is therefore thrilling to find that the English teachings of Jesus on love, forgiveness, and the meaning and purpose of our lives are so intuitive and so effective! They work. They work easily and well. And when they are consistently applied, they build in us new habits of forgiving, loving, and seeking what is peaceful and positive in every situation. They very much improve our whole lives.

Children know as they are applying these teachings that they feel right. And if we help them use the Gospel teachings to form their first habits in dealing with others, they won't establish fear-based and negative reactions that they will have to un-learn later on!

The Gospel Teachings as They are Given in *The Fun of Meeting Jesus*

You might want to read the words that Jesus spoke and compare them with the words in this book. To read them in context, simply buy a modern English translation of the Bible that prints the words of Jesus in red letters. To assist you, here are references to the verses that underlie the words spoken by Jesus in this book.

Page 14

Jesus says: **"Hello children! Come to me. Don't be afraid!**

What Jesus says in the Gospels is:

"Permit the children to come to Me; do not hinder them; for the kingdom of God belongs to such as these" (MK 10:14).

"Do not be afraid, little flock, for your Father has chosen gladly to give you the kingdom" (LK 12:32).

Page 18

Jesus says: **"I am Jesus, the Son of Man. Come and sit with me, children. I love you as God loves you."**

In the Gospels we find him saying:

"**When you lift up the Son of Man, then you will know that I am he, and I do nothing on my own initiative, but I speak these things as the Father taught me**" (JN 8:28).

"**Take courage, it is I; do not be afraid**" (MT 14:27).

Page 20

Jesus says: "**Quentin did not mean to make you lost. Forgive him. If you forgive others, then you will be forgiven when you make your own mistakes.**"

The Gospel words of Jesus are these:

"**Do not judge so that you will not be judged. For in the way you judge, you will be judged; and by your standard of measure, it will be measured to you**" (MT 7:1-2).

"**For if you forgive others for their transgressions, your heavenly Father will also forgive you**" (MT 6:14).

Peter said, "**Lord, how often shall my brother sin against me and I forgive him? Up to seven times?**" Jesus said to him, "**I do not say to you, up to seven times, but up to seventy times seven**" (MT 18:21-23).

Page 24

Jesus says: "**Blessed are the peacemakers. They are doing God's work. Bless you, Emme, that you try to make peace!**"

Jesus says in his Sermon on the Mount:

> "Blessed are the peacemakers, for they shall be called children of God" (MT 5:9).

Page 26

Jesus says: **"Soon I will take you home. But first, let me help you grow in wisdom. All people should be as gentle as children, for the gentle will inherit the earth. The winner is not the one who fights! The winner is the one who lives in love and kindness."**

Jesus often uses children as examples of spiritual perfection. He says:

> "Come to Me, all who are weary and heavy-laden, and I will give you rest. Take My yoke upon you and learn from Me, for I am gentle and humble in heart, and you will find rest for your souls. For My yoke is easy and My burden is light" (MT 11:28-30).

> "Permit the children to come to me. Do not hinder them, for the kingdom of God belongs to such as these. Truly I say to you, whoever does not receive the kingdom of God like a child will not enter it at all" (MK 10:14-15).

> "Blessed are the gentle, for they shall inherit the earth" (MT 5:5)

Page 28

Jesus says: **"People are happiest when they make others happy. Happiest of all are the pure in heart! They live with God."**

Here again are beautiful, timeless words from the Sermon on the Mount:

> "Blessed are the pure in heart, for they shall see God" (MT 5:8)

Page 30

Jesus says: "God is Love. God is Spirit. God is within you, Quentin. You will know God more as you grow."

The words of Jesus about the genuine God are beautiful and timeless:

"You shall love the Lord your God with all your heart, and with all your soul, and with all your strength, and with all your mind (LK 10:27).

"God is spirit, and those who worship Him must worship in spirit and truth" (JN 4:24).

"The kingdom of God is within you" (LK 17:21).

Page 32

Jesus says, "We must love God with all our hearts, just as God loves us. And God wants us to love all people! Love everyone as much as I love you."

Here is God's command that we love, as Jesus expresses it:

"'You shall love the Lord your God with all your heart, and with all your soul, and with all your mind.' This is the great and foremost commandment. The second is like it, 'You shall love your neighbor as yourself'" (MT 22:37-39).

"A new commandment I give to you, that you love one another, even as I have loved you, that you also love one another" (JN 13:34).

Page 34

He says to Quentin, **"You are good to care for your sister and your friends. Be merciful to them. When you show others mercy, you bring mercy to yourself."**

He adds, **"Children, the words that I have spoken to you are from God. Remember them! They will help you to live your best life."**

Jesus's Gospel words are beautiful and timeless:

"Blessed are the merciful, for they shall receive mercy" (MT 5:7).

"It is the Spirit who gives life; the flesh profits nothing; the words that I have spoken to you are spirit and are life" (JN 6:63).

Page 36

Jesus says, **"Dear children, you are the light of the world! Be perfect, as your heavenly Father is perfect."**

Living by the teachings of Jesus impels us to become beautiful examples to others:

"You are the light of the world" (MT 5:14).

"You are to be perfect, as your heavenly Father is perfect" (MT 5:48).

Page 38

Jesus says: **"I am with you always. Seek me and you always will find me."**

Jesus makes it clear in the Gospels that he will forever assist us in following his teachings:

"I am with you always, even to the end of the age" (MT 28:20).

"Ask, and it will be given to you; seek, and you will find; knock, and it will be opened to you" (MT 7:7).

Page 40

Jesus says: **"Remember to forgive with your whole heart! Love everyone the way that I love you! Grow in wisdom, dear children. I am with you always!"**

Here is what Jesus says in the Gospels:

Peter asked him, **"Lord, how often shall my brother sin against me and I forgive him? Up to seven times?"** Jesus said to him, **"I do not say to you, up to seven times, but up to seventy times seven"** (MT 18:21-23).

"This is My commandment, that you love one another, just as I have loved you" (JN 15:12).

"I am with you always, even to the end of the age" (MT 28:20).

The Gospel words of Jesus on love, forgiveness, the nature of God, the nature of humankind, and the meaning and purpose of our lives are among the most beautiful ever spoken. As you become more familiar with them, you will find it ever easier to help your child grow spiritually. And you may find, as I have, that soon you will be doing some wonderful growing yourself!

Beginning to Transform the World

We know that the world is in desperate trouble. From dysfunctional governments and displaced peoples and economic rot in many countries, to violence and the threat of violence and the ever-present threat of a nuclear war, we have lived on a precipice above disaster for so long that it begins to feel normal to us now. But it is not normal. And unless we can begin to address the fundamental rot at the heart of modern Western culture, there doesn't seem to be a way for us to arrest our long slide into barbarism.

So the most important reason for us to be sharing the Gospel teachings with our children is that those teachings have the power to transform our world for the better in one generation. Yes, there are other ways for people to grow spiritually, but most of them are more complicated and they require a significant investment of time. By contrast, the Gospel teachings are simple! And they require so little time that when adults apply them, positive changes often can be seen within months. When as few as five percent of the people on earth are living the Gospel teachings of Jesus, we will begin a benevolent cycle of loving growth and transformation over all the earth. So not only does teaching our children to live the teachings of Jesus much improve their own lives, but it enables each of us to do our part to finally and forever begin together to make a peaceful and love-filled new world.

www.ingramcontent.com/pod-product-compliance
Lightning Source LLC
Chambersburg PA
CBHW050806220426
43209CB00088BA/1653